ZONE

by
Kimberly Chambers

0 43422 70022 6

PHONE AND ADDRESS

_____

_____

_____

_____

_____

_____

_____

_____

_____

Cover and Interior Illustrations by
Design Dynamics, Glen Ellyn, IL
Typography by Roy Honegger

Published by Great Quotations Publishing Co.,
Glendale Heights, IL

ISBN 1-56245-235-5

Printed in Hong Kong

PHONE AND ADDRESS

To my Mother and Father,
dedicated education professionals,
and to my husband, Robert.

PHONE AND ADDRESS

_____

_____

_____

_____

_____

_____

_____

_____

_____

_____

Congratulations on purchasing the "Teacher Zone" calendar, complete with humorous teacher traits, interesting tips, fun things for the holidays and memorable quotes from students.

This calendar was created to brighten your days and provide you with some crafts and activities for you to adapt to your specific classroom environment and grade level. I hope you will enjoy it throughout the year!

PHONE AND ADDRESS

_____

_____

_____

_____

_____

_____

_____

_____

_____

PHONE AND ADDRESS

_____

_____

_____

_____

_____

_____

_____

_____

_____

_____

PHONE AND ADDRESS

_____

_____

_____

_____

_____

_____

_____

_____

_____

_____

PHONE AND ADDRESS

_____

_____

_____

_____

_____

_____

_____

_____

_____

_____

PHONE AND ADDRESS

_____

_____

_____

_____

_____

_____

_____

_____

_____

_____

PHONE AND ADDRESS

_____

_____

_____

_____

_____

_____

_____

_____

_____

_____

PHONE AND ADDRESS

_____

_____

_____

_____

_____

_____

_____

_____

_____

_____

PHONE AND ADDRESS

PHONE AND ADDRESS

_____

_____

_____

_____

_____

_____

_____

_____

_____

_____

PHONE AND ADDRESS

_____

_____

_____

_____

_____

_____

_____

_____

_____

_____

Grow plants in both sunlight
and darkness to show how
light affects plant growth.

December 31

PHONE AND ADDRESS

_____

_____

_____

_____

_____

_____

_____

_____

_____

Select fables to read to the class
that teach an important lesson
and discuss the moral.

December 30

New Year's Day

You know you're a teacher if...

you resolve not to make any
New Year's resolutions.

January 1

Ask students to make a book
illustrating things they could
do to help their parents.

December 29

Teacher's Funny Features:

You have the ability to
look up at just the right
moment to catch students in
the act of passing notes.

January 2

Teacher's Funny Features:

Your bumper sticker says,
"Honk if you like APPLES!"

Teacher ZONE

Watch science shows to
identify scientific experiments
you can perform in class.

January 3

Ask students to write a "'Twas the night after Christmas" story telling what Santa did on the following day.

December 27

You know you're a teacher if...

your own children ask
for permission to go
to the bathroom.

January 4

Teacher ZONE

Use an ant farm in the classroom to illustrate the concept of a community.

December 26

Quirky Quotes from Kids:

"I brought you some make-up my mom doesn't use any more."

January 5

Christmas

Have fun decorating
Christmas cookies!

December 25

Turn the lights out as a signal
for the class to be quiet.

January 6

Teacher ZONE

Mix up the names of popular
Christmas carols and have
students arrange them properly.

December 24

Teacher's Funny Features:

Chalk is your writing instrument of choice.

January 7

Write and decorate
letters to Santa Claus.

December 23

Teacher ZONE

Plan a spring bake sale or
a car wash as a fundraiser.

January 8

See how many words students can make using the letters in "Merry Christmas". For example, "stir", "mister" and "is".

December 22

You know you're a teacher if...

your experience with costume
design is limited to stapled paper
bags and colored construction paper.

January 9

Make and decorate stockings
from construction paper.

December 21

Quirky Quotes from Kids:

"Teacher, what are those
purple lines on your legs?"

January 10

Ask each student to bring a wrapped gift to exchange with another classmate. To control costs, ask them to bring a gag gift and distribute the gifts in a creative way.

December 20

Once a month, have an international day to discuss different countries and their cultures. Ask students to watch the news for any current events taking place in the country you discuss that month.

January 11

Make reindeer ornaments by gluing together three clothespins—two with the "legs" pointing down, and one with the "antlers" pointing up. Finish by adding plastic eyes and a felt nose. Reindeer can also be made by gluing pipe cleaner antlers, eyes and a nose to a candy cane.

December 19

You know you're a teacher if...

your favorite ink color is RED!

January 12

Bring holiday foods from different countries to share with the class.

December 18

Choosing helpers of the week
to assist in distributing handouts
and collecting homework can make
unmotivated students feel involved.

January 13

Teach a lesson on how Christmas is celebrated around the world.

December 17

Teacher ZONE

You know you're a teacher if...

you have perfected
"the look"—guaranteed to
stop kids dead in their tracks.

January 14

Teacher ZONE

School Paste

Organize a trip for the school choir
to sing Christmas carols in a
local hospital or nursing home.

December 16

Discuss the important messages of
Martin Luther King in honor of his
birthday and the contributions of other
African American leaders in history.

January 15

Record the class singing
Christmas carols.

December 15

You know you're a teacher if...

you put cute little stickers on
your husband's work reports.

January 16

Collect socks and gloves to
donate to needy children.

December 14

Teacher ZONE

Discuss the many inventions of
Ben Franklin and review his sayings
in the *Ben Franklin Almanac*.

January 17

Make up hand signals for
favorite Christmas carols.

December 13

Teacher ZONE

Teacher's Funny Features:

Your favorite hobby is seeing
how many crafts you can
make from popsicle sticks
and empty milk cartons.

January 18

Teacher ZONE

Decorate gingerbread houses and display them throughout the school. Submit a house from either each student, class, or grade level and judge to see who wins the first prize! Ask a local theater to donate tickets for the winner.

December 12

You know you're a teacher if...

you sing the "ABC song" as you
look up words in a dictionary.

January 19

Decorate the class tree with paper ornaments and paper chains or popcorn strings for garland.

December 11

Discuss the significance of taking
an oath or making a promise
for *Inauguration Day*.

January 20

Collect small gifts such as powder,
lotion, magazines and teas to
give to nursing home residents.

December 10

Quirky Quotes from Kids:

"Do I get extra points for turning the assignment in on time?"

January 21

Teacher ZONE

Have a school-wide door decorating contest.

December 9

Teacher ZONE

You know you're a teacher if...

you have to get glasses twenty
years too early from having to
read the microscopic answers
in the teacher's edition.

January 22

Select a story to read to
the class which conveys
the meaning of giving.

December 8

Teacher's Funny Features:

You receive a note saying,
"What do mean you can't read my
son's handwriting?" in handwriting
that's worse than the child's.

January 23

Teacher ZONE

Quirky Quotes from Kids:

"Here's your fruit cake, teacher. We got it last year for Christmas."

December 7

Teach a lesson on how to use
the telephone book, including
the residential, business
and government pages.

January 24

You know you're a teacher if...

over half of the ornaments on
your Christmas tree read,
"To My Teacher"!

December 6

Teacher ZONE

Ask for a volume discount
at the teacher's supply store.

January 25

Remove key words from famous
Christmas stories or carols and
have students fill in the correct
word and label the part of speech.

December 5

Teacher ZONE

Have students make their own
telephone book of important
telephone numbers for their
relatives, police, fire, poison control
and their parents' work numbers.

January 26

Teacher ZONE

School Paste

You know you're a teacher if...

you're actually used
to hearing fingernails
scratching a chalkboard.

December 4

Teacher's Funny Features:

You feel like you have
eyes in the back of your
head to catch troublemakers.

January 27

Teacher's Funny Features:

Your students faint when they
see you in the store in your
worst pair of sweats.

December 3

Keep extra Valentine's Day cards
on file in case someone
doesn't receive as many.

January 28

Contact the fire department and request a fireman to teach students fire safety tips. Follow up with a field trip to a fire station.

December 2

Give out a homework pass to skip a homework assignment as a reward for being on time, being well-behaved or following instructions.

January 29

Teacher ZONE

You know you're a teacher if...

spit wads come out of your
hair when you shower.

December 1

You know you're a teacher if...

your idea of an evening of culture
is going to the school play.

January 30

You know you're a teacher if...

you constantly correct the
speech of others.

November 30

Teacher ZONE

Quirky Quotes from Kids:

"Why did you take off points just because my paper was late?"

January 31

Teacher ZONE

Have students cut a picture from
a magazine in half, paste it to
a sheet of construction paper,
then draw the missing half.

November 29

Incorporate lessons on African American history and bring in library books featuring African Americans throughout the month of February in honor of Black History Month.

February 1

Teacher Zone

Teacher's Funny Features:

You are thankful for the
Thanksgiving Holiday!

November 28

Groundhog Day

Discuss how customs, rituals, superstitions and myths impact everyday life.

February 2

Teacher ZONE

Design Pilgrim and Native American costumes using construction paper and brown paper bags. Make collars and hats with buckles for the Pilgrim costumes out of construction paper. Decorate vests, dresses and headbands with feathers made from brown paper bags for the Native American costumes.

November 27

You know you're a teacher if...

every adult you meet reminds
you of one of your students.

February 3

Teacher ZONE

Create a bartering activity in the classroom to show how Pilgrims and Native Americans traded based on their desire for items such as corn, meat and fish.

November 26

You know you're a teacher if...

you always have a hole in the big toe of your hose from kids stepping on your foot.

February 4

Ask students to draw a picture
of one thing they are thankful for.
Display the drawings to remind
everyone of all the different reasons
to celebrate *Thanksgiving*.

November 25

Consider sponsoring a flower sale
for Valentine's Day as a fundraiser.

February 5

Contact a Native American
organization and request a speaker
to inform students about their Native
American culture and heritage.
Ask them to bring special items
such as costumes, tools or
artwork for students to view.

November 24

Teacher Zone

Teacher's Funny Features:

You stop wearing perfume because the smell of permanent markers has deteriorated the lining of your nose.

February 6

Teacher's Funny Features:

You never have to finish
the sentence that begins,
"If I hear you talking
one more time…"

November 23

Teacher ZONE

Teach a lesson on how to use telephone automated information systems. Make a tape for students to listen to, then have them diagram the menu choices.

February 7

Teacher ZONE

Ask students to bring different vegetables from home to make a vegetable soup in class for lunch.

November 22

You know you're a teacher if...

your desk is full of junk as a result
of the "If I see that one more
time it's mine" threat.

February 8

Teach a lesson on the health hazards of smoking or ask the school nurse to give a presentation in honor of the *Great American Smokeout,* which occurs on the third Thursday in November.

November 21

Distribute a list of student names so
that kids can address Valentine's Day
cards to their classmates.

February 9

You know you're a teacher if...

before you use a napkin,
you check to see if
there's a retainer inside.

November 20

Teacher ZONE

You know you're a teacher if...

you wake up to your alarm clock thinking there's a fire drill.

February 10

Throw your state a birthday party on the anniversary of its statehood. Discuss the official state bird, tree, flower and logo. Have students design a new state license plate.

November 19

Have students list everything electric in their home and teach a lesson on the impact of electricity in honor of Thomas Edison's birthday.

February 11

You know you're a teacher if...

both your house and wardrobe
feature "ABC" decor.

November 18

In honor of Lincoln's Birthday, make a log cabin by removing the top of an empty milk carton, and gluing tooth picks onto all of the sides. The cabins can also be painted brown for an authentic look.

February 12

Have students bring dominoes to class, then set up a giant winding display and watch them fall. Follow up with a math lesson on how to keep score in domino games.

November 17

Teacher ZONE

Have students decorate and attach small paper bags to their desks in order to collect cards during the exchange on Valentine's Day.

February 13

You know you're a teacher if...

you inadvertently tell your
friends to spit out their gum.

November 16

Teacher ZONE

Valentine's Day

Make silhouettes of each student as a Valentine's Day gift to parents. Have the student sit in front of a projector so that you can trace their profile. Cut out the profile from a black sheet of paper and mount it on a white background.

February 14

Set up a paper recycling
bin in your classroom.

November 15

Teacher ZONE

You know you're a teacher if...

you have your own orchard of wooden and ceramic apples.

February 15

Quirky Quotes from Kids:

"I missed the bus because it left my stop too early."

November 14

Make a family tree on construction
paper and add apples to list
the family members.

February 16

Teacher ZONE

Encourage students to participate in events and reading clubs at participating local bookstores. Ask the bookstore to provide a class discount card to students.

November 13

Teacher's Funny Features:

You just love it when a raised hand is accompanied by a chorus of "Ooh! Ooh! I know! I know!"

February 17

Teacher ZONE

You know you're a teacher if...

you have to go to restaurants
outside the five mile radius of
your school to enjoy happy hour.

November 12

You know you're a teacher if...

you never leave home without
your automatic slide grader.

February 18

Contact the local veterans association
to request a speaker prior to or
immediately following *Veteran's Day*.

November 11

Teacher ZONE

Have students memorize the names
of all of the Presidents of the
United States and make a book of
Presidential trivia for Presidents' Day.

February 19

Teacher ZONE

Quirky Quotes from Kids:

"Do readin', ritin'
and rithmitic' all start
with the letter 'r'?"

November 10

You know you're a teacher if...

your greatest fear is getting
a speeding ticket in your
own school zone.

February 20

Teacher's Funny Features:

In-service days are
always your favorite.

November 9

Ask a local merchant to donate
supplies or equipment, such as
a computer, to your school once
you have collected store receipts
from parents totalling an
agreed upon amount.

February 21

Teacher ZONE

SCHOOL BUS

Ask craft stores for extra materials or donations to be used on classroom projects.

November 8

Teacher ZONE

Review George Washington's achievements and make Martha Washington candy in honor of Washington's birthday.

February 22

Quirky Quotes from Kids:

"Is it cheating if my mom uses a calculator when she does my math homework?"

November 7

Teacher ZONE

You know you're a teacher if...

you remind your friends to be
courteous by asking,
"What do you say?" when
they forget to say thank you.

February 23

You know you're a teacher if...

you correct the spelling in red
on that lovely letter from
Aunt Bea and return it.

November 6

Have students make their own
jigsaw puzzle. First, draw a
picture on a piece of cardboard,
then cut it into irregular puzzle pieces.
Trade with friends and put
them back together.

February 24

Hold a mock election to illustrate the voting process for *Election Day*, the first Tuesday in November not dated the first. Ask the local polling area to bring a machine to your school before or after the official elections for use in your mock election. Based on your class' or school's results, try to predict the results of the real election.

November 5

Keep a bank of bonus questions
on file in case you want to add
a little spice to your tests.

February 25

Initiate a canned food drive
contest between other classes.

November 4

Teacher Zone

Assign a book report to be written
as book jacket, with art work on
the front, back and spine, and
a summary on the inner flaps.

February 26

Use a classroom calendar to
convey a theme for the month.

November 3

You know you're a teacher if...

the smell of a stink bomb
no longer fazes you.

February 27

You know you're a teacher if...

you have a great sense of smell—
you can smell trouble or
a rat a mile away.

November 2

Teacher ZONE

Organize a mock debate to illustrate the importance of seeing both sides of an issue.

February 28/29

Teacher ZONE

Contact the local hospital to see if they will bring a candy scanner to your school to check Halloween candy.

November 1

Let students describe themselves and their interests in a collage made of magazine clippings in honor of National Youth Art Month.

March 1

Halloween

Turn out the lights in the classroom, light candles and tell ghost stories!

October 31

Teacher's Funny Features:

You know "Teacher, I need to…" is always followed by a request to go to the restroom.

March 2

Turn an empty classroom into a haunted house! Let one class design the haunted house using large cardboard boxes to make mazes, and fill bowls with grapes for eyeballs and noodles for brains. Limit participation to older students, and require a parental permission slip.

October 30

You know you're a teacher if...

you find it hard to participate in adult conversations after you've been around kids all day.

March 3

Ask a police officer to speak about trick-or-treating safety guidelines.

October 29

Make a tape of songs that mention
the names of places in the lyrics,
then have students identify the city,
state or body of water on a map.

March 4

Vote on jack-o-lantern designs
displayed in the classroom and
carve a pumpkin in class
using the winning design.

October 28

Teacher ZONE

Teacher's Funny Features:

No one can sit in the back seat of your car because it's filled with teaching materials.

March 5

Once you know the date ending
daylight savings, don't forget to
remind students and teach them
the reasons for having
daylight savings time.

October 27

Teacher ZONE

Maintain a class checkbook to teach addition, subtraction and the importance of budgeting for the unexpected.

March 6

Teacher ZONE

Put a spooky Halloween tree with dead branches on the bulletin board, then let students make decorations such as pumpkins, bats, witches and ghosts.

October 26

Teacher ZONE

You know you're a teacher if...

the book you safeguard the most is your gradebook, not your checkbook.

March 7

Take a field trip to a local market
to buy a class pumpkin.
Afterwards, design jack-o-lanterns
on construction paper and use
them to decorate the classroom.

October 25

Teacher ZONE

Have a set of newspapers delivered to the school and teach a lesson on how to read a newspaper and find articles in various sections.

March 8

In honor of *United Nations Day*, have each student draw and decorate a flag from a different country.

October 24

Teacher ZONE

Teacher's Funny Features:

The words you hate to hear the most are, "My mom wants a parent–teacher conference."

March 9

Ask a volunteer with a seeing eye
dog to explain or demonstrate the
functions the animal performs.

October 23

Teacher ZONE

Quirky Quotes from Kids:

"Teacher, my dad forgot
to bring my lunch."

March 10

Teacher ZONE

Ask a sign language volunteer to demonstrate in your class and teach students the sign language for a song.

October 22

Teacher ZONE

Contact the Wall Street Journal
for information on the
special classroom edition
of their publication.

March 11

Teacher ZONE

For *Handicapped Awareness Week*, the third week in October, ask your special education department to provide handicapped sensitivity training to your class. Have students role play individuals with different handicaps.

October 21

You know you're a teacher if...

some of your favorite artwork
is done in crayon.

March 12

Devote a lesson to personal safety.

October 20

Teacher ZONE

Decorate the classroom with
shamrocks decorated
by each student.

March 13

Have a class camp-in to reward the class. Ask students to bring picnic foods and set up tents made from sheets in the classroom.

October 19

Teacher's Funny Features:

You strain your back every time you bend over to drink out of the kid's water fountain.

March 14

Teacher's Funny Features:

You shop on the other
side of town to avoid
students and their parents.

October 18

Teacher ZONE

Hold a career day, inviting parents or other professionals to teach students about their occupations.

March 15

Teacher ZONE

Let the kids make shaving
cream designs on their desk.
When they wipe it off,
the desks are clean!

October 17

You know you're a teacher if...

you've wiggled more
loose teeth than a dentist.

March 16

On National Bosses Day, remind your principal to thank you for starting the fearful rumors about being sent to the principal's office!

October 16

Teacher ZONE

SCHOOL BUS

St. Patrick's Day

Have a "Who Can Be Seen
in the Most Green" contest.
The student (or teacher)
wearing the most green wins!

March 17

On *National Poetry Day*, have
a poetry contest by writing
a limerick or a haiku.
Read the winning submission during
the morning announcements.

October 15

Teacher ZONE

Quirky Quotes from Kids:

"My dad said I was accidentally overlooked for the gifted program."

March 18

Have students bring political
cartoons to class and
discuss their meaning.

October 14

Teacher ZONE

Challenge pairs of friends in a game by asking one partner to second guess what their friend would answer to questions asked by the rest of the class while the friend is in the hallway.

March 19

Teacher ZONE

You know you're a teacher if...

you always carry a
disguise in your car.

October 13

Teacher's Funny Features:

You're used to being asked "What page are we on?" halfway through the lesson.

March 20

Teach a lesson on explorers and compare them with modern space explorers in honor of *Columbus Day*.

October 12

Divide students into groups and act out fables or nursery rhymes.

March 21

Teacher ZONE

Teacher's Funny Features:

You're willing to "duke it out" to see who gets the student teacher.

October 11

Teacher's Funny Features:

Your portrait is commissioned annually—by the school photographer.

March 22

Randomly place a lucky
sticker on a handout, and
award the winner a prize.

October 10

Teacher ZONE

Hold a creative writing contest.

March 23

Teacher ZONE

Quirky Quotes from Kids:

"My mom forgot to
bring my homework."

October 9

You know you're a teacher if...

you have perfected the art of hearing without listening. ("Uh-huh…" Pause. "Uh-huh…")

March 24

For *National Children's Day*,
explain why so many people
and politicians stress that
"the children are our future"

October 8

Illustrate the use of statistics by polling
the class on a particular subject,
then showing them how to compute
a ratio. Also, show a pie chart
or bar chart and relate statistics
to the grading system.

March 25

You know you're a teacher if...

"open house" means meeting
parents instead of putting
your home on the market.

October 7

Teacher ZONE

You know you're a teacher if...

your favorite times of the day
are the same as the kids:
recess, lunch and gym.

March 26

Teach a lesson on star identification for the appropriate season before organizing a trip to the planetarium.

October 6

Teacher ZONE

SCHOOL Paste

Pair new students with a different partner each day for a week to help them make friends and learn their way around.

March 27

Teacher Zone

Make "hamburgers" in class.
Use vanilla wafers for buns,
chocolate cookies for meat,
red icing for ketchup and
green icing for lettuce.

October 5

You know you're a teacher if...

your idea of being well read is
having completed the latest
children's book series.

March 28

Quirky Quotes from Kids:

"My parents said you should help us learn the material instead of giving us so much homework."

October 4

Quirky Quotes from Kids:

"Is this going to be on the test? Because if it's not, I must not need to know it."

March 29

To prepare students for an exam, hold a trivia contest between groups of students using questions the students submitted.

October 3

Teacher ZONE

Create some games to practice
telling time and remind
students when daylight
savings changes the
time in the spring.

March 30

You know you're a teacher if...

every important paper
you own is laminated.

October 2

You know you're a teacher if...

the clerks in the local craft
store know you by name.

March 31

Request a volunteer to teach
business issues from organizations
such as Junior Achievement.

October 1

Teacher ZONE

April Fool's Day

Organize a school-wide "Backwards Day", where students and teachers wear their clothes backwards and inside-out, to celebrate April Fool's.

April 1

You know you're a teacher if...

you begin to count to three
when people in the movie
theater are being too noisy.

September 30

Teacher ZONE

Decorate Easter eggs made
of construction paper and
hang them from the ceiling
of the classroom.

April 2

Teacher's Funny Features:

The .01% at the bottom
of your pay stub was the
amount of your last raise.

September 29

Teacher ZONE

You know you're a teacher if...

you've had every childhood
illness known to man.

April 3

Teacher ZONE

Learn a new vocabulary word by writing it on the chalkboard every day.

September 28

Teacher ZONE

Have an Easter extravaganza
complete with an egg hunt,
egg toss and an egg relay,
using a spoon to carry the egg
to the next team member.

April 4

Teacher's Funny Features:

Your students are so thrilled
to see you in the grocery store,
they make sure everyone
knows you're their teacher!

September 27

Count the number of candy pieces
used to fill a jar. Ask students to
guess the correct number of pieces.
The guess closest to the
correct number wins!

April 5

Designate one day of the week to discuss current events from newspaper clippings students bring to class.

September 26

Make fuzzy bunnies or chicks
by gluing cotton balls onto
outlines on construction paper.

April 6

You know you're a teacher if...

you know the name of every
crayon color in the jumbo box,
but you can't remember the last
time you had a "night off".

September 25

Teacher ZONE

Decorate real Easter Eggs!

April 7

Ask local restaurants to sponsor parties for your class. In return, your students can make posters and craft projects for the restaurant to display to show their community involvement.

September 24

Teacher's Funny Features:

You begin marking off the days until summer vacation.

April 8

Teacher ZONE

Teacher's Funny Features:

Your favorite oxymoron
is the lounge, where
you actually scarf lunch in
less than ten minutes.

September 23

Make a class patchwork quilt with a
decorative border around squares
designed by students. If you can't
sew it yourself, ask a parent or
friend who sews to volunteer.

April 9

Teacher ZONE

You know you're a teacher if...

you have bad circulation in your
arms from writing on the chalkboard
and varicose veins in your legs
from standing all day.

September 22

Teacher's Funny Features:

You take simple precautions in life, such as an unlisted telephone number and a locking gasoline cap.

April 10

Choose 12 art pieces that
students have designed and
make a class calendar.

September 21

Partner with a younger grade to facilitate learning. One example is a reading buddy program in which the older student writes a story for a younger student and uses it to help the younger student practice reading.

April 11

You know you're a teacher if...

you can fill in a
scan-tron bubble perfectly
with your eyes closed.

September 20

Quirky Quotes from Kids:

"My mama saw you driving the other day, and she said you drive like a bat outta somewhere."

April 12

Teacher ZONE

Review the Bill of Rights during *Constitution Week*, the third week in September.

September 19

You know you're a teacher if...

you never miss a comment made
behind your back due to your
supersonic hearing ability.

April 13

Teacher's Funny Features:

You know exactly who other teachers are referring to when they say, "Do you have *HIM* in class this year?"

September 18

Teacher's Funny Features:

You keep a collection of your
favorite notes from parents.

April 14

Emphasize the many freedoms
we have as citizens of such a
great country for *Citizenship Day*.

September 17

Ask the local police department to give a presentation on bicycle safety. Some police departments sponsor bike identification programs, so don't forget to ask if your students can register their bikes with the police after the presentation. *National Bike Safety Week is designated as the third week of April.*

April 15

Teacher Zone

Teacher's Funny Features:

You wonder if the instructions on giving the achievement test are harder than the questions.

September 16

Teacher ZONE

Teacher's Funny Features:

Substitute teachers can identify troublemakers by the marks you have by their names.

April 16

Quirky Quotes from Kids:

"The dentist said my tooth is infected. Wanna see?"

September 15

Find out if a local bank or credit union is sponsoring a student contest for *National Credit Week*.

April 17

Teacher ZONE

Create a class scrapbook
for students to maintain
during the year.

September 14

Teacher ZONE

SCHOOL BUS

Quirky Quotes from Kids:

"You should take an aspirin
for your headache.
My dad says they're great
for hangovers, too."

April 18

Teacher ZONE

You know you're a teacher if...

you appreciate simple privileges
of life, like going to the
restroom in private.

September 13

Ask a policeman to give a
presentation on stranger
dangers and fingerprint
all students.

April 19

Place a marble in a jar every time the class is behaving well. Take one out when they are misbehaving. When they accumulate 20 marbles, have a class party.

September 12

Teacher's Funny Features:

You dread teaching a
difficult subject after
lunch or recess.

April 20

Teacher ZONE

You know you're a teacher if...

your first name ceases
to exist—instead you are
given the title "Mrs." whether
you're married or not!

September 11

Teacher ZONE

You know you're a teacher if...

you've given out more
autographs than a movie star—
on arm and leg casts, that is.

April 21

Make a collage with photos
of children with their
grandparents to give to the
grandparents as a present.

September 10

Teacher ZONE

Contact the city to obtain information
and materials on recycling, and teach
a recycling lesson for Earth Day.
Have a contest to see which class
collects the most recyclable material.

April 22

You know you're a teacher if...

when people take more than ten items through the express lane, you ask if it's because they can't read or they can't count.

September 9

Teacher ZONE

You know you're a teacher if...

you think you should register
pop-quizzes as deadly weapons.

April 23

Teacher ZONE

Ask kids to write letters to their grandparents or tape record an interview with them for *Grandparent's Day.*

September 8

Teacher Zone

Don't forget your school secretary during secretary's week which occurs during the last full week of April. *Secretary's Day* is the Wednesday of that week.

April 24

Quirky Quotes from Kids:

"My mom said you color your hair. Do you use crayons or markers?"

September 7

Teacher's Funny Features:

Your idea of torture:
  a) School lunches
  b) Teacher workshops
  c) Year-round school
  d) All of the above

April 25

Teacher ZONE

Organize a before-school breakfast allowing students to bring their grandparents to celebrate *Grandparent's Day*, which falls on the first Sunday after *Labor Day*.

September 6

Plant a tree on the school grounds or donate a tree to a local park in honor of *Arbor Day*, the last Friday of April.

April 26

Teacher's Funny Features:

You realize that you have to take a number to use the school telephone.

September 5

Quirky Quotes from Kids:

"Teacher, I didn't know
you could wear shorts!"

April 27

Have students complete an information
sheet at the beginning of the school year.
Be sure to include a question asking parents
if they have any special talents or
knowledge they would like to present in
their child's class, or if they would serve
as a volunteer story reader.

September 4

You know you're a teacher if...

you always have more than
ten rulers in your top drawer.

April 28

Teacher ZONE

You know you're a teacher if...

every pen you own
contains red ink.

Teacher ZONE

Ask a nursery for donations to plant a flower bed or garden on the school grounds. Take a field trip to the nursery so they can demonstrate proper planting procedures.

April 29

Explain why we observe *Labor Day*, which is the first Monday in September, either before or after the holiday occurs.

September 2

Teacher's Funny Features:

Your worst school photo ends up being memorialized in the school yearbook.

April 30

Teacher Zone

Contact the state and request a
list of local and statewide events
for the upcoming year.

September 1

Teacher ZONE

Sponsor a zoo animal in honor of
Be Kind to Animals Week, which
occurs during the first week of May.
Also, display pictures of pets
on the bulletin board.

May 1

You know you're a teacher if...

you put smiley faces
on your personal checks.

August 31

You know you're a teacher if...

you have the ability to elicit fear
just by saying a student's first
and middle name.

May 2

Play name bingo to help students learn the names of their classmates. Have students write the names of 16 classmates on a piece of paper with a 16 square grid. Students then cover up the names with a piece of cereal when a name is called. Whoever completes a column, row, or diagonal first wins!

August 30

Teacher ZONE

Find out the date for
"Take Your Child to Work Day"
and encourage parents and
children to participate.

May 3

Teacher's Funny Features:

When students ask if they "can"
do something instead of if they "may",
you reply, "I don't know, can you?"

August 29

Quirky Quotes from Kids:

"My dad said this homework was a complete waste of time, just like the parent–teacher conference you had with him last week."

May 4

Teacher ZONE

Send parents a craft collection sheet asking for items to be used in making crafts, such as buttons, empty milk cartons and empty egg cartons.

August 28

You know you're a teacher if...

you start telling strangers to "sound the word out".

May 5

Teacher's Funny Features:

If you had a dollar for every apple you've been given…

August 27

Teacher's Funny Features:

You keep "post-recess potpourri"
in your classroom to
freshen the air.

May 6

Teacher ZONE

Get to know students and have fun on the first day of class with an "ice breaker"! Without disclosing the purpose of the game, ask students to pass around a roll of toilet paper and tear off as many sheets as they would like. Once everyone has counted their pieces, they must tell something about themselves for each piece taken.

August 26

Have a kite flying day with homemade or store-bought kites, complete with a contest for whose kite flies the highest or doesn't get stuck.

May 7

Teacher's Funny Features:

You could write a book
on homework excuses.

August 25

Teacher ZONE

Teacher's Funny Features:

You leave a list of tasks you want
to avoid for the substitute
teacher to complete.

May 8

You know you're a teacher if...

the vent on your
clothes dryer is full of chalk
dust from your clothes.

August 24

Quirky Quotes from Kids:

"Don't you wish you had a kid just like me!"

May 9

Assign research projects on the
history of your town or community.
Display the projects in the school
and invite community leaders
to view them.

August 23

Teacher ZONE

Make a recipe book for mom
for a *Mother's Day* gift.

May 10

Teacher ZONE

You know you're a teacher if...

you cut better with
safety scissors than with
regular adult scissors.

August 22

You know you're a teacher if...

you have more power in your
pointer finger than a super hero.

May 11

Develop a list of class rules to review with students at the beginning of the school year and post the rules at the front of the room.

August 21

Teacher ZONE

Don't forget to call mom on *Mother's Day*, the second Sunday in May.

May 12

Teacher's Funny Features:

Your clothes are stretched from children tugging on them to get your attention.

August 20

Quirky Quotes from Kids:

"Just because my dad spelled his name wrong on my report card doesn't mean he's not the person that signed it."

May 13

Teacher ZONE

Make paper airplanes to
celebrate *Aviation Day* on
August 19. Award a prize
to the plane that flies the greatest
distance and discuss the impact
made by the Wright brothers.

August 19

Teacher ZONE

Have a concert in class! Let kids make their own noise maker and bring it to class for a concert. Divide into rhythm and string sections and don't forget the aspirin!

May 14

Teacher Zone

Teacher's Funny Features:

You buy tissues by the case to prepare for the runny nose season.

August 18

You know you're a teacher if...

when you have trouble breathing,
you wonder if your lungs are
filled with chalk dust.

May 15

See if there are any videos, like
safety videos for latch-key children,
at the local library or video store
that you would be interested
in showing your class.

August 17

Have the author of a children's book
present the book to several schools.
Divide the author's fee with
the other schools.

May 16

Teacher's Funny Features:

You're not sure who
dreads the first day of school
more—you or the students.

August 16

Write a class thank you card
to parents who volunteered
during the year.

May 17

Begin each day by sharing
a positive saying or an
inspirational quote with the class.

August 15

Teacher ZONE

School Paste

Ask a member of the armed
services to explain why we
observe *Armed Forces Day*, the
third Saturday in May, and the
upcoming *Memorial Day* holiday.

May 18

Teacher ZONE

You know you're a teacher if...

you use peanut butter to get
chewing gum out of hair more
than you use it to make sandwiches.

August 14

Quirky Quotes from Kids:

"Homework, busy work, what's the difference?"

May 19

Teacher ZONE

If you have access to a computer, evaluate some of the new software packages developed to manage grade recording and averaging. The expense may be offset by the time you could save!

August 13

Organize a school Playday on the
playground or at a local park
with athletic events and adult
sponsors. Try incorporating
an Olympics theme for fun.

May 20

You know you're a teacher if...

you tell students to look it up
before they can finish saying,
"How do you spell...?"

August 12

Quirky Quotes from Kids:

"Teacher, I think I'm about
to throw... blahh!"

May 21

Make noodle jewelry such
as necklaces and bracelets
by stringing different shapes
of pasta together. Non-toxic
paints can also be used for
more colorful jewelry.

August 11

Teacher Zone

Hold a mock graduation in class at the end of the school year.

May 22

You know you're a teacher if...

you tell your spouse,
"Because I said so!"
when he/she asks why.

August 10

Teacher ZONE

Teacher's Funny Features:

Your favorite item in "Show and Tell" is Uncle Buck's set of false teeth.

May 23

Suggest that students keep a diary
or journal of their thoughts.
Not only does it help them express
their feelings, it's fun to read years
later when they are older.

August 9

Teacher ZONE

SCHOOL BUS

Make a piece of impressionist art. Color a picture with crayons on the grainy side of a piece of sandpaper, then place the sandpaper face down and iron it onto construction paper. The heat will transfer the picture onto the construction paper.

May 24

You know you're a teacher if...

instead of a letter, you send
corrections to the editor
for every newspaper and
magazine article you read.

August 8

Teacher ZONE

You know you're a teacher if...

you have two voices—
your own and your
teacher voice!

May 25

Discuss the important role family plays in everyone's life to help students feel good about their immediate and extended families.

August 7

Teacher ZONE

Bring baby pictures to school
and see who can identify
the most students.

May 26

Teacher ZONE

Send a postcard the week before school to each student in your upcoming class. Tell them about yourself and welcome them to your class!

August 6

Obtain information to teach students about *Memorial Day*, the last Monday in May.

May 27

You know you're a teacher if...

your fingerprints have been
worn off from writing on
and erasing the chalkboard.

August 5

You know you're a teacher if...

an assigned seating chart
is your weapon of choice.

May 28

You know you're a teacher if...

your August ailment is
Back-to-School Blues.

August 4

Teacher ZONE

List a brain jogger on the board for students to solve when they complete their assignment early. For example, the solution to "88 K on a P" is 88 keys on a piano, and "7 D in a W" is seven days in a week.

May 29

Play pictionary on the chalkboard with spelling words or vocabulary words to reinforce the correct spelling and definition of each word.

August 3

Find out if there is a list
of local merchants offering
teacher discounts.

May 30

You know you're a teacher if...

unlike most adults,
you can name the capital
of all fifty states.

August 2

Have students make a collage of
all the food groups with magazine
pictures to reinforce nutrition lessons.

May 31

Teacher's Funny Features:

You begin your "back to school countdown" for the month of August.

August 1

You know you're a teacher if...

you have trouble naming your own
children because every name you
think of reminds you of a student.

June 1

You know you're a teacher if...

your own children raise their
hands to ask you a question.

July 31

Teacher ZONE

Practice mock interviewing to prepare students for interviewing for a job or leadership position.

June 2

Teacher ZONE

Check the school calendar for
long weekends and plan
your vacations in advance.

July 30

You know you're a teacher if...

you think the real achievement is administering the achievement tests.

June 3

Quirky Quotes from Kids:

"Here's my homework. My mom said you wouldn't be able to tell the difference in her writing versus mine."

July 29

Take instant photos during field trips and place them on the bulletin board once you return. Have students write a story about the pictures displayed.

June 4

Price spelling or vocabulary words
by assigning values to letters.

July 28

You know you're a teacher if...

June, July and August
are your favorite
months of the year!

June 5

Teacher's Funny Features:

No gum chewer
goes unnoticed.

July 27

Ask the high school art department to draw a giant map of the United States on the school parking lot to allow students to walk through states they are studying. Decide on non-permanent chalk or permanent paint depending on whether or not you want to keep the map for the following year.

June 6

You know you're a teacher if...

your favorite song is the "ABC" song.

July 26

Teacher ZONE

Have a rephrase day.
Pass out negative sayings and
have another child rephrase it
in a nicer, more polite way.

June 7

You know you're a teacher if...

you have calluses on
your fingers from filling in
scan-tron bubbles.

July 25

Teacher's Funny Features:

You wonder how you made it before anti-hyperactive medication.

June 8

Trade bad habits on paper and
come up with ways to improve.

July 24

Teacher ZONE

SCHOOL BUS

Develop a list of personal projects
to complete during the summer.

June 9

You know you're a teacher if...

you've given more tests than
a product development
laboratory has.

July 23

Teacher's Funny Features:

If the kids only knew those last
six assignments didn't count
because you averaged
their grades early!

June 10

You know you're a teacher if...

the numbers on your
calculator are worn off
from averaging grades.

July 22

Teacher ZONE

Obtain an origami book and
let students make different
designs to be displayed
in the classroom.

June 11

Teacher ZONE

Quirky Quotes from Kids:

"Here are some flowers I picked for you from my neighbor's garden."

July 21

You know you're a teacher if...

you wish you could
threaten to send adults to
the principal's office!

June 12

Explain the important role
of blood banks and explain
the reason for having
blood drives.

July 20

Make an "Appreciation Book" to
give to Dad on *Father's Day*!
On each page, students should
draw a picture of something
Dad does for them
that they appreciate.

June 13

Teacher ZONE

SCHOOL BUS

Collect empty shoeboxes so
the class can make their
own shadowboxes.

July 19

Flag Day

Create a colorful version of Old Glory in honor of Flag Day. Have students cut red, white and blue tissue paper into one inch squares. Then, place the eraser end of a pencil in the center of the square and twist the sides around the pencil. Glue the flat end of the tissue square onto the flag in the appropriate colored section and remove the pencil.

June 14

You know you're a teacher if...

you say, "Excuse you,"
to those who forget to
excuse themselves.

July 18

Teacher Zone

Raffle class art work and let the winning student take it home.

June 15

Plan a exercise on telling time in different time zones using airline schedules. For example, ask students what the flying time is if you depart Dallas, Texas at 2:00 pm, and you land in New York City at 6:00 pm.

July 17

Have students make a collage
of pictures of their dad to
give to him for *Father's Day*,
the third Sunday in June.

June 16

You know you're a teacher if...

you've heard the phrase,
"Teacher, do you remember me?"
over a million times.

July 16

Organize an anti-drug campaign
for your class or school.

June 17

Make cupcake cones to decorate
in class with icing and toppings.
Don't forget, *National Ice Cream
Week* occurs the week in July
containing the fifteenth.

July 15

Request local newspapers to list school contest winners for recognition.

June 18

Quirky Quotes from Kids:

"My parents said you should
be evaluated by our test
scores instead of your ability."

July 14

Quirky Quotes from Kids:

"Teacher, Robert has some little bugs in his hair, and we all used his comb."

June 19

Plan a western or 50's
dress-up day for fun.

July 13

Teacher ZONE

Have students make a resumé of the things they do well as a self-esteem builder.

June 20

Establish an on-going class project for students to work on in their free time.

July 12

Contact a sports figure from a
professional team to speak
at a school function.

June 21

Teacher ZONE

You know you're a teacher if...

you know the location
of every craft and office
supply store in the city.

July 11

You know you're a teacher if...

you hear, "I don't know how!"
over 50 times a day.

June 22

Prepare a lesson on the birthstone
and flower of each month.

July 10

Teacher ZONE

Teach a lesson or ask the school
nurse to present information
on proper dental hygiene.

June 23

Publish a school newspaper
with interviews from kids
and sell copies for
a fundraiser.

July 9

Teacher ZONE

Hand out a lengthy questionnaire with the first instruction being, "Do not fill out this form," to teach the importance of reading directions.

June 24

Teacher ZONE

You know you're a teacher if...

the width of your shoe
increases every year
from standing all day.

July 8

Teacher's Funny Features:

You'd love to meet the smarty-pants who first prompted classes to say, "Good Morning, Teacher."

June 25

Teacher ZONE

SCHOOL BUS

Decorate a class sheet
with fabric markers.

July 7

Contact the local weather
channel to obtain programs
on dangerous weather.

June 26

Quirky Quotes from Kids:

"My daddy wants to know
if you're married?"

July 6

Teacher's Funny Features:

You considered volunteering
to tutor in your spare time,
then you woke up.

June 27

Teacher ZONE

Ask the electric company to present a program on safety around electricity. Also, find out if they have any special promotional contests for students during the school year.

July 5

Build a model or replica
of a local business. Some
businesses may award prizes
for community awareness.

June 28

Independence Day

Teach a lesson on the history of fireworks and the many reasons they are used.

July 4

Always reward perfect attendance.

June 29

Quirky Quotes from Kids:

"What do I get for
doing my homework?"

July 3

Quirky Quotes from Kids:

"My parents said you shouldn't get a raise because you already get paid for doing nothing in the summer anyway."

June 30

Hold math problem races on the chalkboard, or play math baseball with each correct answer counting as a hit.

July 2

OTHER CALENDARS BY GREAT QUOTATIONS

365 Days Of Life In The Stress Lane
365 Reasons to Eat Chocolate
Apple A Day
Baby Boomer Blues
Beauty Secrets
The Candy Counter
Champion Quotes
The Dog Ate My Car Keys
Each Day A New Beginning
Fortune Cookies - Without The Calories!
Friends Forever
Generations
Golf Forever…Work Whenever
Good Living
The Heart That Loves Is Always Young
Home Is Where The Heart Is
Home Sweet Home
How To Speak Fluent Child
I Think My Teacher Sleeps At School

Keys To Success
Kid Bits
Kind Words…Softly Spoken
A Kiss of Sun
Mrs. Webster's Daily Dictionary
Never Never Give Up!
Our Thought For The Day
Quick Tips for Home Improvement
Quotes From Great Women
Real Friends Are Hard To Find
Seasonings
Secrets Of A Successful Mom
Simple Ways To Say I Love You
Simply The Best Dad
Simply the Best Mom
Stretching Your Dollars
Teacher Zone
Teachers Are "First Class!"

OTHER BOOKS BY GREAT QUOTATIONS

Cheatnotes On Life
Fantastic Father, Dependable Dad
For Mother - A Bouquet of Sentiments
Global Wisdom
Growing Up In TOYLAND
Inspirations
Interior Design For Idiots
Let's Talk Decorating
Mrs. Aesop's Fables

Mrs. Murphy's Laws
Mrs. Webster's Dictionary
Mrs. Webster's Guide To Business
Parenting 101
Romantic Rhapsody
The Secret Language Of Men
The Secret Language Of Women
A Teacher Is Better Than Two Books
TeenAge Of Insanity

Decorate placemats and use
them to control messes
when serving snacks.

July 1